HEALING MYSTERIES

A Scriptural Rosary

Adrian Gibbons Koesters

Paulist Press
New York/Mahwah, N.J.

Imprimatur:
+Most Reverend Eldon J. Curtiss, DD
Archbishop of Omaha
May 10, 2004
Nihil Obstat: Reverend Michael F. Gutgsell
Moderator of the Curia, Archdiocese of Omaha, Censor Deputatis.

The Imprimatur is the Church's declaration that a work is free from error in matters of faith and morals, but does not imply that the Church endorses the contents of the work.

The Scripture quotations contained herein are from the New Revised Standard Version Bible: Catholic Edition, Copyright © 1993 and 1989 by the Division of Christian Education of the National Council of the Churches of Christ in the United States of America. Used by permission. All rights reserved.

Cover design by Cynthia Dunne
Illustrations by Julie Lonneman

A plenary indulgence, under the usual conditions, is granted to those who pray the Rosary.

Library of Congress Cataloging-in-Publication Data

Koesters, Adrian Gibbons.
    Healing mysteries : a scriptural rosary / Adrian Gibbons Koesters.
       p. cm.—(IlluminationBooks)
    Includes bibliographical references.
    ISBN 0-8091-4299-6 (alk. paper)
    1. Suffering—Prayer-books and devotions—English. 2. Rosary. I. Title. II. Series.
    BV4909.K62 2005
    242'.74—dc22

                                        2004022083

Published by Paulist Press
997 Macarthur Boulevard
Mahwah, New Jersey 07430

www.paulistpress.com

Printed and bound in the United States of America

Contents

In Memoriam

Dedicated to Rose Fitzpatrick Copenhaver,
Frances Stauch Gibbons,

Josephine Mueller Koesters,
and Mary Boylston Mehuron,

and to Francis P. Sullivan, SJ,
and Thomas Lukaszewicz, SJ

Preface

The greatest gift we receive from God during our lives is not simply the gift of love, but the gift of learning how to love. Everyone experiences setbacks in how they are able to receive and use this gift; among these setbacks are experiences of chronic illness and traumatic injury, which, often more than anything else, isolate us and turn us in on ourselves. This book is presented as one way for people who have, for whatever reason, lost their inner connection to the Holy Spirit. It is the Spirit who leads us to love ourselves as we are, who helps us to join in communion with our brothers and sisters, and who challenges us to care for the created world in which we are called to fully live.

Prayer is a vital way to regain and maintain our connection to God and the world. The prayer offered here uses three separate scripture accounts of healing found in the Gospel of Mark. Following the prayer form of the Rosary, a single scripture story is entered into deeply, using what St. Ignatius called "active contemplation." Each story attends to one of three ways in which we all need healing, regardless of our life experiences: healing of physical wounds, healing of our emotional and spiritual wounds and the blindness which often results, and finally, ultimate healing from death, as we find fulfillment of that most vital promise of new life. As you pray, then, you will literally put yourself in the place of the one whom Jesus heals, turning your eyes, ears, and heart toward Jesus and asking him to lead you through the healing story.

I have prayed the Rosary in this way for more than ten years and have found it powerful in my own healing journey, helping foster a growing relationship with Jesus and Mary, and giving me the ability to reconnect to the world. It is significant that since this book was begun, Pope John Paul II has introduced the fourth Luminous Mysteries, focusing on the public ministries of Jesus. I hope that the meditations on the public healings of Jesus offered here are seen as a complement to that holy and sustaining prayer.

Acknowledgments

I would not have written this book without the early encouragement of Elaine Jachyra, with whom I originally discussed the idea. I am most grateful to Mary Helen Stefaniak, director of the creative writing program at Creighton University, who read the original manuscript and made invaluable suggestions for its improvement. Thanks also to Carolyn Meeks of the Adult Formation Office of the Archdiocese of Omaha, who commented on an early draft. Lawrence Boadt, CSP, publisher at Paulist Press, provided an essential focus and sequence for the text, and I am exceedingly grateful for his confidence in the manuscript. Paul McMahon, managing editor at Paulist, provided constant support and kindness. I am most grateful to Kevin di Camillo, editor at Paulist, for his invaluable direction and support during the production of the book. Thanks also to colleagues at Creighton University, past and present, especially James Datko, OMI, Eugene Selk, Jack Walsh, Leonard Greenspoon, Rose Hill, Ronald Simkins, Frances Minear, Mary Beth Bestenlehner, Joan Howard, and Barbara Angus. Many thanks to Hélène Mercier, OSB, Oblate director for the Monastery of St. Benedict, St. Joseph, Minnesota; to Maureen Crouchley and Richard Hauser, SJ, directors of the Creighton Christian Spirituality Program; and to Bert Thelen, SJ, pastor of St. John's Church in Omaha, and Rita Sherman, adult formation director at St. John's. My sisters, Monica Rose and Cecily Updegraff, shared in the journey. Finally, to my husband Mark and daughter Clare, my deepest love and gratitude.

Introduction

I collect rosaries: stainless-steel finger rosaries; crystal First Holy Communion rosaries; plastic glow-in-the-dark rosaries; olive wood rosaries; and even a beautiful bright-green ceramic rosary with a Celtic cross (made, of course, in Italy). I keep them in my bedside table drawer, my handbag, my car, my coat pockets, and my laundry room. Early memories of being in church include listening to the soft whoosh and slide of rosaries pulled out of a pocket or case, and their sharp clink against the church pews before the beginning of Mass or after receiving absolution in the confessional.

The sound and feel of rosary beads resides deep within my physical and spiritual memory, yet for a long time I did not pray the Rosary at all. Like others of my generation, I was not familiar with the richness of the contemplative tradition of the Church. Rather than understanding how vital a part of this tradition the Rosary is, I perceived it as an outdated piety. Even so, I often had no problem praying the prayers of other religious traditions—often using beads! It was during a period of chronic illness that began more than a decade ago when I gradually—and very uncertainly—began to gather rosaries. It took some time after that to actually begin praying the Rosary in its traditional form, and even later before the meditations in this book took shape.[1]

Before I introduce these meditations, it may be helpful to reflect generally on how wounds to the body and psyche affect the spiritual life. I would like to briefly describe experiences and reflections during more than two decades of healing the effects of trauma and living with a chronic illness, as it was in this context that I was first inspired to pray with these scriptures using the Rosary.[2] The observations that follow have specifically to do with the effects on the spirit and prayer after trauma or illness. The last section of this chapter, "Before You Begin," offers some guidelines and assistance if it has been some time since you have engaged in prayer or if you are currently in a delicate physical or emotional state. Then, when you move to the meditations themselves, pray any of the healing mysteries that speak most directly to you.

How Trauma Affects the Spiritual Life

The experience of traumatic injury due to abuse or catastrophe is one with which many of us are greatly familiar. The events of September 11, 2001, alone exposed many thousands more people, especially in the United States, to the immediate and lasting effects of experiencing or witnessing such trauma. These traumas not only serve terrible wounds to the body and mind, but to the sufferer's ability to connect with the greater community and to God.[3] If these are not healed, the outcome is nearly invariably isolation and despair. For some of us, despite outward signs that we are functioning well in the world, elements of this despair resist healing. Most of us gradually heal from bodily wounds, and as improvements continue to be made in the psychological and behavioral treatment of survivors of trauma, with proper care our functioning and ability to rejoin our families and communities can now be greatly restored. Yet we may still live with a deep emptiness, unable to name it, unable to talk about it with others, a feeling that there is still something essential in us that is broken, unable to be touched, much less brought to wholeness.[4]

It is true that many people live with pain, and many people know times of despair. Yet for those of us who have experienced traumatic injuries, especially if these result in a disconnection with family or the larger community, what has often been taken away are the reminders of our natural and innate ability to know God as ever-present, completely loving, and always ready to be with us, despite the outward hardships we live through.[5] We also lose the perspective that suffering in this life is not the last word, and that, for whatever reason we experience suffering and illness, God has not forsaken us.

For Christian believers, the mystery of the Cross is evidence that God is with us in the worst we experience, but being fragile and having limitations, we lose our ability to enter into that mystery. We come to a place where we are convinced that God will surely save everyone else, but we can't imagine that we are worth saving. We project our feeling or experience of abandonment onto God. We can well relate, even as Jesus did, to the anguish expressed by the opening cry of Psalm 22: "My God, my God, why have you forsaken me?" In praying these meditations, you are encouraged to remember that in the same psalm, these words of suffering are in dialogue with the essential promise of our faith: "Yet it was you who took me from the womb; you kept me safe on my mother's breast" (v. 9); and, "The poor shall eat and be satisfied"(v. 26).

Our tendency to become stuck in a place of darkness is especially strong if we experienced trauma early in life, when our thoughts had a magical and concrete character. We perceived consequences as the direct result of our "goodness" or "badness," and our childlike image of God was fixed as one of the punisher or the rewarder. These convictions about our identity, our very character, take root in the soul and become cemented there; they become a block to happiness and emotional ease, one we "just can't get at," no matter how hard we try. Although we may come to a conscious understanding that what troubles us is a hidden (albeit untrue) conviction that we are unlovable, even "bad to the core," those early convictions hold powerful sway over our imagination. Even as we may come to believe that our loved ones do care for us, and we may get better in every other way, we cannot let go of the shame and fear we hold onto in the face of God. We hold to a tenacious and misunderstood impediment to experiencing the presence and love of God.

Chronic or severe physical illness is another wounding that can lead us to despair of the love of God. Our self-image is usually deeply connected to the ways we contribute to society or provide for our loved ones, or how we are able to care for and pay attention to them. When we become disabled, our loved ones, friends, and colleagues seem to not know who we are anymore. We ourselves can begin to feel invisible. At the same time, we also don't want to "draw attention to ourselves." Worst of all, if we try to reach out for help, we may be rebuffed by people unable to fully understand our predicament because they have not yet experienced similar losses.

Unfortunately, we often comply with this state of affairs by putting a brave face on things (at least in this way we are still protecting and taking care of those we love!). The result: we experience loneliness at a depth we hardly imagined could exist. We try everything to "fix it"; like the woman healed of her hemorrhage, we "use up all our resources" to get ourselves back in working order. We even try to put on a brave face for God as a sort of bargaining chip (because we believe that God, like the rest of the world, will only heal us and be true to us if we're up and running, "in good shape").[6]

Aging can also contribute to this sense of useless-ness and invisibility. At some point, the middle-aged or older person usually experiences the shocking awareness that others have literally stopped seeing them—they have become a kind of "walking wallpaper" in the rooms of life. Worse, they often experience this from those to whom they have been closest in their lives. Even in the absence of any other wounds, this loss can be devastating, especially since we have done nothing to cause it except continue to live. At the mercy of what are no more than cultural blind-ers, we often personalize and internalize the experience. It may anger us, but, again, trying to "fix" reality by stoically pretending it doesn't exist, we can sink into profound depression.

In the course of any of these experiences, it is depression that usually adds a terrible insult to injury. It is the nature of depression, described as an inner mechanism that robs our feelings of their vitality,[7] to introduce and reinforce the distorted conviction that there is something wrong with us: "I am poured out like water, and all my bones are out of joint" (Ps 22:14). We pray, but our prayer comes to lack a necessary quality of comfort and hope.[8] We seek healing, but continue to wonder what real healing might mean. We have glimpses that Jesus is with us, but they are fleeting. We are in darkness; we need something to hold onto until the light comes again. We try to follow the way of the Cross, but find we don't have the strength or energy to be the Simons of Cyrene we desire to be. In short, the consequences of our physical or psychic illness manifest in the depths of our souls: how can we live with this blackness, this continual need to say to God, "I cry by day, but you do not answer; and by night, but find no rest" (Ps 22:2).

Moreover, as we go through these experiences, it can easily happen that others become upset with us if we timidly (or even angrily) reach out for help. They may look at our problem as something we should "get over"; worse, they may not be shy about telling us to "get over ourselves." Even if we wanted to follow such advice, it is hard to understand how we could go about it. Isolation grows, resentment grows, and distorted perceptions become our reality. More than anything, we need help to interrupt this cycle of being and perceiving. It is at precisely this point when we need to turn to Jesus in prayer.

Therefore, let us gently and compassionately make a new beginning. We need to remember that we were created by intention, that our life task is to become who God wants us to be, to learn as fully as possible what it means to love. So let us begin to explore, especially in prayer, how, far from wishing us to become other than who we are, God has created us uniquely and beautifully. This is easy to strive for when we are feeling whole, connected, and healthy; how hard it is to recall in our moments of fragmentation, isolation, and illness! The temptation is hopelessness: we are alone, God is not with us, we are helpless. Giving in to this temptation can also be the easy way to deal with our pain. The harder course is to admit and trust in the truth that, despite our suffering, we also have a real source of comfort and solace.

Understanding the difficulties we may have to live with, let us still try to make the return to what has become hidden in our minds: that despite outward appearances, despite inner loneliness, God is with us. God intends for us to know wholeness even in our worst suffering. Waiting for us to turn to him, God is ready and willing to walk with us all the way. If we can do this, even if our steps are small and unsure, we can rediscover our essential selves and return to lives of wholeness and communion.

When we seek out the true companionship Jesus waits to give us, there are no guarantees about how strangers will see us, or that loved ones will become more patient with our difficulties. But we hope that what will change is how we see ourselves and how we experience the reality of the healing, saving, and risen Lord. We can begin to hope that our sense of self will be renewed and our inner strength restored. As our hope grows, our ways of finding new sources of healing will grow with it.

Some religious traditions refer to the Lord as "The Friend." It was in the course of praying these mysteries that I found comfort and healing from deep losses, and how in great part I was able to rediscover friendship with Jesus and his compassionate mother, Mary. As you begin this journey of hope and reconnection of your friendship with the Lord, may this prayer of healing be for you a part of that promised restoration and renewal.

Why a Healing Rosary?

Praying with the Rosary with other than the traditional mysteries is nothing new. For example, there are many "chaplets" in existence, specific prayers using or built around the Rosary; among the most well-known today is probably the Chaplet of the Divine Mercy. It is the physical form of the Rosary itself that is so helpful in making the life and work of Jesus real to those who pray it. The Rosary can have a profound impact on those of us who, as a result of illness or injury, have experienced blocks in our prayer and relationship with God precisely because the physical world has come to seem unreliable or unreal.

The "advantage" of the Rosary, if you will, is that it is one of the most concrete, physical ways of praying that we have. For persons suffering from illness of the body or heart, "holding on" is a literal need as well as a figurative one. Simply holding the Rosary during difficult times, even when prayers don't easily rise to our lips, is indescribably comforting and grounding. On the days that we would rather stay sick, stay with what we know, at the point when we feel stuck in an unbreakable cycle of discouragement, we can be astonished at how so simple an act as holding onto a string of Rosary beads can act as the bridge we need between our pain and the rest of reality. Praying the Rosary can then lead us gradually and gently forward into health and wellness, to reconnection with the Spirit and the world.

The Focus of the Healing Mysteries

The traditional Rosary makes use of a potent tool that anyone can use, the act of imaginatively entering into life with Jesus. In this book, we will use the format of the Rosary to pray into and past our own negative experiences by using three powerful stories of healing found in the Gospel of Mark, in a progression that also mirrors our development and maturation in the life of faith.

1) The first meditation, "Jesus Heals the Wounds of Our Body," guides us into the story of the healing of the woman with the hemorrhage (Mark 5:25–34). The meditations that accompany this scripture focus on the healing of physical trauma and illness, as well as the healing of wounds to the spirit and the loss of a sense of self that so often result. You may find, especially at first, that you most naturally gravitate to this story about healing the body, mind, and heart of physical (including sexual), psychic, and spiritual wounds. Here we are praying the prayer of Jesus on the Cross, asking him with the same confidence with which he called out to the Father, to ease our pain, to take away our distress and our hopelessness. We confirm in our minds, our hearts, and especially our bodies how close Jesus always is to us. We rediscover the boundless desire of Jesus to heal us in every way. We let that desire into our hearts, to settle in our thoughts, and to ease our suffering in whatever way God means healing to come about in our lives at this time.

2) The second meditation, "Jesus Opens Our Blindness," explores the healing of the blind man at

Bethsaida (Mark 8:22–26). We come to "see" how, when we are overwhelmed or despondent, we are so readily blinded to the power of the Spirit within us and the presence of God around us. We meditate on how our inability to see or our fear of true sight keeps us from acknowledging God's power to transform us. Gradually, our eyes are opened to our own strength. We hope to find in God's grace the ability to open our eyes to the truth that we have a part in God's plan to further his kingdom. We no longer need to lapse back into the easy comfort of "enjoying" our poor health. Safe with Jesus, our eyes opened to his vision, we accept that even we, weak as we are, have been given the power to act with and for Jesus to usher in the reign of his Father. This is challenging and certainly it can be frightening, but once it happens, like the blind man we can't help but embrace it with arms open, praising God at the tops of our voices. You may find that it takes a long while to approach this meditation or believe that it can even remotely apply to you, but take your time, be patient and gentle with your needs, and see how you are moved by it.

3) The final meditation, "Jesus Raises Us to New Life," guides us through the raising of Jairus's daughter (Mark 5:22–24, 35–43). Here we not only recollect God's promise to raise us from physical death, but we also pray for the grace to waken from whatever sleep we are in now, a sleep we are tempted to when pain keeps us from seeing life as the gift that it is. This is both a gentle story and a challenging one. We all need to wake up to our own adult place in the world. We are all tempted to remain sleeping when life's demands are or seem overwhelming. When we

are hurt or become ill, the temptation to stay asleep or to try to numb the pain of sickness (especially if we compare it to what looks like the abundance of others) is all too great. In this meditation, Jesus helps us to know that he is with us in the same way a loving, tender, and patient Father is with his young daughter. This daughter, standing on the threshold of life, is "petrified" by the dawning awareness of what hurts may come when she is forced to take her place in the world. Jesus reassures her that it is safe to get up. He reassures and reminds us that life is completely good, that it is completely ours to partake of, and that, despite outward pain and discouragement, we are completely protected within his love.

The Method of This Prayer

Each story is designed to be prayed as a five-decade sequence, but if you wish, you may pray a single decade at one sitting, entering deeply into the meditation for that decade. Further, it is not necessary to pray each set of decades in the sequence they are presented here. Since each addresses a different need, you may find that you return to one story more than the other two over a period of time. The most important thing to remember is to put your own imagination to work as you pray in order to experience the healing and companionship of Jesus, and this, of course, will change as your needs and awareness change.

If you are used to praying the traditional format, you will notice that one essential difference in this Rosary is that each "mystery" or miracle of healing is a single story divided into five parts, one part to be prayed with one decade. Each mystery begins with a preparatory reflection. This is followed by five decades beginning with a scripture verse, followed by a meditation, and ending with the usual sequence of Rosary prayers for the decade. As you pray these prayers, try to imagine Jesus accompanying you on a journey of healing and growth. As you progress, allow the Spirit to guide you.

To begin, simply pray in the traditional way, beginning with the Sign of the Cross and the Apostle's Creed (the full format of the Rosary is found in the Appendix). Praying the Hail Mary strengthens our friendship and devotion to Mary, who accompanies us with her son as Mother of Compassion and Health of the Sick. If we haven't known a physical mother who has been a comfort and support to us, this experience is also a powerful one.

From time to time I have also prayed the Jesus Prayer ("Lord Jesus Christ, Son of the living God, have mercy on me") in place of the Hail Mary. Use the formats and meditations here as a starting place, and adapt them as your unique needs and inspiration lead you.

Before You Begin

In general, find a quiet place to pray where you will not be interrupted. Some people like to pray while lying on their backs, but if you are unused to prayer, it may be helpful at the beginning to sit upright in a comfortable chair with your feet flat on the floor. Falling asleep is a natural tendency, so at first try to physically arrange yourself so that it becomes less of a problem. You want to be relaxed, but not completely relaxed! Beginning with a few deep breaths is helpful, and as you pray, try to breathe from your abdomen, as the more shallow breathing most of us do can cause anxiety, or deepen it if it is already present.

Many people like to close their eyes during prayer, but if you prefer, another helpful method is to focus on a spot on the floor a few feet in front of you, your eyes about half-way open.[9] What is best is whatever helps you to visualize the scene, enter into it, and focus on Jesus during your prayer. A crucifix or icon of Jesus, images of Mary, candles, and quiet instrumental music nearby are all helpful and comforting aids to prayer.

Above all, be patient, kind, and nurturing to yourself. Prayer is not (or at least it shouldn't be) a kind of spiritual Olympic games. You are building a friendship and trust with Jesus, and like all good friendships, this takes time. You may find that praying a single decade will be more than enough to lead you into prayer. Be generous with yourself, with your moods and lapses (although it is more helpful to pray as regularly as you can), and don't force much at the beginning. Your intentions will bear fruit as you begin this new relationship with Jesus and his Mother.

Now, let us begin. May the peace and healing of Jesus Christ which passes all understanding be with us, as we begin this journey with him.

PART ONE

Jesus Heals the Wounds of Our Body

The Healing of the Woman with the Hemorrhage. (Mark 5:25–34)

Opening Reflection

Chronic illness or the lifetime scars of the wounds of abuse often feel invisible, as if no one sees them, much less understands the pain they cause. In moments of darkness we make bargains with God: "Take this away from me and I'll turn my life over to you." We go underground, hiding in our suffering, or we become false martyrs, using our illness to punish others.

But behind all our defenses, behind all our strategies, there is a pain that drives us: a need to be seen, to be touched, to be healed by the God who holds our suffering as well as our healing in the palm of his hand. In this scripture, a woman who has probably suffered for most of her

adult life sees Jesus and decides to approach him. An unfathomable risk!

She comes humbly, jeopardizing her reputation and perhaps even her faith—the outcome could be "nothing" once again—simply to touch his robe. She can't even imagine, as Paul says, what Jesus has ready for her. It's so far beyond her ability to envision and believe, but she is willing to take the first step.

As you begin to pray this healing mystery, put yourself there as if you are this person. Imagine yourself in the crowd. Get ready to take this first step, make this first response. Imagine your sensations: your eagerness, your desire to make a change in your way of living. You hope against hope that someone is there for you in your need. Begin your prayer knowing that Jesus is just there, just within reach, waiting for you to touch him. Understand that what you seek is only a fraction of the promise Jesus has in store for you.

The First Decade

> Now there was a woman who had been suffering from hemorrhages for twelve years. She had endured much under many physicians, and had spent all that she had; and she was no better, but rather grew worse. She had heard about Jesus, and went up behind him in the crowd and touched his cloak. (Mark 5:25–27)

Meditation

Many of us have spent hundreds or even thousands of dollars on myriad therapies in search of healing, and still we are often not much better than when we started. Sometimes we're blamed when we don't get well. Other times, we seek healing but we want to skip the process and arrive at the moment where "it's all better." In the meantime, the people in our lives may expect us to be silent or still (or both) until that time. If we have been marked by suffering and illness, those have become the focus, the big screen onto which we project all our experiences. The images of suffering block out the images of healing and hope, but those are the ones we now have to get ready to see.

As you begin this decade, let the feelings brought on by your illness or wound gently come into consciousness. Be aware of the pain, discomfort, or disease that hurts you. Like the woman, feel how hopeless things have been; remember how much energy and how many resources you have spent on trying to get well. Now imagine Jesus is just in sight. Pray for the grace to see only him, just there, just within reach. Imagine you are coming up to Jesus in the crowd and taking the risk to be near him and touch him. Let your thoughts, sensations, and images fully be here, in this place, with him.

Pray one Our Father, ten Hail Marys, one Glory Be.

The Second Decade

For she said to herself, "If I but touch his clothes, I will be made well." (Mark 5:28)

Meditation

What an assertion for this woman to make! She is not only sick in body and poor in resources, but the fluid issuing from her body also makes her an outcast. To think that to be made well she should touch a rabbi is utterly outside the limits of normal judgment. She takes this leap of imagination, but stops there. She is used to asking for so little: she'll just touch his garment; she will get what she wants from Jesus without "really" touching him.

We are so like her: we feel less worthy than the person we need to reach out to, and even in our pain we want to let the one who can help us off the hook. Some of us suffer from diseases that make us unclean in our own society, to our own family and friends. How could Jesus possibly feel differently about us than we do about ourselves? Like this woman, we hope *not* asking will bring us what we need, that we won't have to get anyone else dirty.

As you pray, feel any shame you have and think about the distress this has caused you. Remember how acting on your shame has wounded the relationships in your life. Now think about the possibility of letting go of shame and what it might mean to have the hope that comes from reaching out. Reflect on how being humble is so different from being ashamed. Now see Jesus again. Look around at the faces of the crowd. Say to yourself, "I know he cares for them; he will care for me." Know that Jesus is near to you and is waiting for you to reach out to him.

Pray one Our Father, ten Hail Marys, one Glory Be.

The Third Decade

Immediately her hemorrhage stopped; and she felt in her body that she was healed of her disease. (Mark 5:29)

Meditation

Immediate healing doesn't happen for most of us, and this becomes another temptation. The thought lingers, beckons to our weakness: If only we were good enough, Jesus would prove his love for us; he would "immediately" cure us. But we live in the reality of the Resurrection, and most of us are no longer called to give witness to Jesus through being cured. Far to the contrary, immediate fixes are now the norm: denial of suffering and death are the fixtures of our consciousness, and fast-food-commercial solutions pollute our spirit. We are challenged to feel in our bodies and believe in our hearts that Jesus is healing us in the way we most need healing, even if not immediate, even if not visible. Rather than our healing, it is our suffering that in many ways is our witness to others; in time it may serve as a grace for others who suffer. We can be part of the healing touch of Jesus in a way that people can hear and believe now, today.

Even with this in mind, still imagine right now that your illness has completely healed. Imagine the fire you feel in your hand as you touch Jesus, and how that burning, healing touch courses through your body. You don't know yet what it means, but you know it is real. Stay with this feeling as long as you can. As you progress through this decade, reflect that, whatever form your "hemorrhage" takes, you are being touched and healed by the loving hand of Jesus in the way you most need it. Trust that reality as you pray this next decade.

Pray one Our Father, ten Hail Marys, one Glory Be.

The Fourth Decade

Immediately aware that power had gone forth from him, Jesus turned about in the crowd and said, "Who touched my clothes?" ...He looked all around to see who had done it. (Mark 5:30, 32)

Meditation

In this moment we can readily imagine the woman wanting to simply turn and run. How well we can identify with that temptation: *Jesus, let me talk to you, but please don't look at me, please don't answer me!* Jesus knows our fear, but he wants us to tell him who we are, or who we think we are. He knows that this wounded self we carry around is no more our real self than the stoic self who won't let on how much it is hurting, how alone it is.

As you begin this decade, remember the meditation of the previous decade. Hang on to the determination to let go of shame; embrace the conviction that it is safe

21

and good to be seen, to be visible and vulnerable. Continue to imagine how perfectly Jesus can be trusted. If you are afraid, imagine too the hope and wonder of the woman in the crowd. Imagine, as she must have, how it seemed as if all the other people fell back, like a curtain she no longer had to push through to talk to Jesus, her healer. See his face as he turns, see his welcome and compassion for the first time, and know that it is all yours. Form the words you wish to tell Jesus, begin to say mentally what soon you'll tell him aloud. Put yourself in his path and finally recognize that he and he alone is the safe haven you have been seeking all this time.

Pray one Our Father, ten Hail Marys, one Glory Be.

The Fifth Decade

> *But the woman, knowing what had happened to her, came in fear and trembling, fell down before him, and told him the whole truth. He said to her, "Daughter, your faith has made you well; go in peace, and be healed of your disease." (Mark 5:33–34)*

Meditation

We don't know what this woman's truth was—sometimes she is confused with the woman taken in adultery (John 8:3–11)—but there is a sense that some sexual shame or something to do with her identity as a woman has caused or contributed to this unceasing hemorrhaging. It is hard to imagine the sheer relief of being able to let go of that much anxiety and then to be able to "tell the whole truth."

For those who have suffered rape or other trauma to their sexual selves, "coming clean" is almost unimaginable; it is always terrifying, and the truth often falls on the ears of people who don't want to or don't know how to help. They may know how to say, "It wasn't your fault." This is certainly better than hearing "It *was* your fault." Still, their words may do little to ease our feelings of shame, guilt, and loneliness. Remember that it was not only telling Jesus the truth that cured this woman, but his word to her in response: "Go in peace, and be healed of your disease." Even as she knelt down in fear and trembling, she was able to "tell him the whole truth."

Now it is time for you to tell Jesus everything. You know what it is to feel that deep trembling of anxiety: imagine yourself there now. Imagine Jesus listening to you with endless patience and boundless compassion. Gently begin to let go of the anxiety, helplessness, and despair that you feel. Know that you *can* tell Jesus everything. Know that he is making you well, and that you will be healed of your "dis-ease." Gently and firmly rest in this trust as long as you can.

Pray one Our Father, ten Hail Marys, one Glory Be.

End the decade by praying the Hail, Holy Queen, or other prayer to the Blessed Virgin Mary.

End of the First Healing Mystery

PART TWO
Jesus Opens Our Blindness

The Curing of the Blind Man at Bethsaida.
(Mark 8:22–26)

Opening Reflection

*T*his story is very short, taking up a bare paragraph, but it reflects the nature of action: after the groundwork is laid, often few words are needed. Jesus comes to the man, asks what his problem is, cures him, and then directs him not to go back where he had been, but to go "home," where he belongs. After other healings, the person often loudly praises Jesus even after he has been admonished to be quiet about what has happened (for example, Mark 7:36). That image is missing here, but we can easily imagine the blind man praising Jesus, at least in his heart, for restoring his sight.

Sight is a profound gift, one that can be physically lost and then restored; we ourselves may know of such healing. I once knew a woman who had been blinded by macular degeneration. After learning that she would gradually go blind, she said, "I have a choice now. I can remain grateful for what I have, or I can decide to become angry, bitter, and helpless. I choose gratitude." She had no expectation of healing, but as it happened, her blindness was healed by prayer. The impact it made on her already-strong felt experience of Jesus and his empowering spirit in her life continued until her death.

As you begin this mystery, perhaps there is a similar person in your own life, living or dead, a witness to the power of God—a person close to you, or a saint or figure from history who experienced this reality. As you pray, imagine that you too can partake of the boundless Spirit of God, and ask him to strengthen your desire to open those places where you are blind to God present in your life. Especially pray for the grace to see where you have been blind in learning how to love.

The First Decade

They came to Bethsaida. Some people brought a blind man to him and begged him to touch him. He took the blind man by the hand and led him out of the village... (Mark 8:22–23)

Meditation

Imagine that you are blind. Now imagine that you are being led by someone you don't know who has promised to take you to "get cured." Instead of being able to direct yourself, to go where you want, or to find the healing or direction that you think will work best for you, you are in someone else's power. You must follow his or her directions and time table. Anyone who has spent any time in a doctor's office or hospital bed knows this experience and has felt the tedium and fear that can accompany it. Often your wishes are not consulted ahead of time, you don't have full information, and you can't "see" ahead to know what is coming next.

Now imagine that you have taken Jesus' hand—and he does the same thing! He leads you away, but you have no idea where the two of you are going. This can't be good! But then you remember who Jesus is: your healer, your protector, and your friend. You can trust that this opening of your blindness is simply another step on the way. As you begin this decade, imagine the darkness, imagine your feet stumbling, your hand being pulled, but feel how different it is from other times when you have had to follow blindly. Imagine an ever-greater sense of confidence; imagine your step growing ever more sure. Feel the strength coming from Jesus, your companion; feel the comfort and absolute assurance that he is there for you.

Pray one Our Father, ten Hail Marys, one Glory Be.

The Second Decade

*...And when he had put saliva on his eyes
and laid his hands on him, he asked him,
"Can you see anything?"* (Mark 8:23)

Meditation

The laying on of hands is the time-honored
method and metaphor for healing. We have been touched
by the Lord, and healing is already taking place. But now
we are being led to see things we have not let ourselves see
before; we are being opened to possibilities that our physical or metaphorical blindness have kept back from us. This
blindness may have been an important defense mechanism
in the past. But Jesus asks us what we see now that we have
been given back the gift of our sight. He wants to know
what we see, and he wants us to tell him.

Enter deeply into your imagination as you pray
this decade, and try to "see" everything that comes to you.
At first, perhaps all you experience are sounds, or smells,
or physical sensations. Yet try to open your mind to visual
images as much as you can. Imagine the slow renewal of
sight, the slow entering of light into your eyes. Does it feel
confusing? Is it painful? What do you see now that Jesus
has touched you? Now, as you begin to see these images
and feel their consequences, begin to tell Jesus what
appears before you. Be deeply aware of your feelings and
sensations as you take this journey of imagination. Further,
imagine what Jesus might be beginning to show you, what
he might now be calling you to, what he might be offering

to you as your authentic vision of the future. Begin to reexperience what is possible, begin to open yourself to what you had not been able to see—or do—before.

Pray one Our Father, ten Hail Marys, one Glory Be.

The Third Decade

And the man looked up and said, "I can see people, but they look like trees, walking."
(Mark 8:24)

Meditation

In our illness, we can often forget that our perception of reality has become distorted by pain and suffering. As we begin to find our way, at first things will surely not appear as they really are. As we progress, we come to find that this challenge—seeing things as they are, rather than as we imagine them to be—is truly is the task of a lifetime. But we begin to see the truth, little by little. We may have been blinded for so long by our pain or illness that seeing the truth of some things is more difficult than others, and we may still imagine other things as they are not. This is where the beginning of discernment takes place, not only now in prayer but also in all aspects of our lives, especially as we become less and less isolated from the world. At this point in the journey, it is vital to find a source of help, a reliable teacher or guide who can help to interpret these new experiences. You will find that, even though things are not clear yet, they will be.

Again, as you begin to pray this decade, imagine how it feels when you cannot quite make out what you are trying to see, and the frustrations that come with it. You sense that eventually things will become more and more clear, but for now you are still "bumping into things" or experiencing things that seem strange to your sight. This can be disheartening—and irritating! Remember, even if you are not as comfortable as you want to be, your clearing vision has deepening power in it. Allow yourself to hope in the sight that you have, and be grateful for the increasing clearness that Jesus is promising to you. Tell him all that you see, as often as you need to.

Pray one Our Father, ten Hail Marys, one Glory Be.

The Fourth Decade

Then Jesus laid his hands on his eyes again; and he looked intently and his sight was restored, and he saw everything clearly. (Mark 8:25)

Meditation

As we move on in our healing and begin to see more and more clearly, we also often find that we begin to see many familiar things differently than we saw them before. Distortions are removed from our sight and our minds. The key in this passage is the phrase "he looked intently." This is hard work, and it is almost never without cost. It is frightening to see the truth, and it takes even more work to remain faithful to it—that is the nature of sight, the nature of truth.

If you feel afraid or unwilling to meet this challenge, it may be in good part because you worry that facing the truth will leave you on your own again. Remember now that Jesus is always and everywhere with you. You are no more alone now than before; the difference is that now you are "looking." The ability to see the truth will not condemn you to more isolation or loneliness than when you were in the dark; in fact, you will be able to see Jesus (and others) with you even more completely than before.

So as you begin to pray this decade, feel your great joy in seeing Jesus for the first time. Imagine how wonderful it is to see him clearly, right there, with you. Imagine the look of joy and welcome on his face, how deeply he rejoices in your new sight. Feel the excitement of sharing the flood of ideas and possibilities you have, now that you no longer stumble. And begin to think about how you now can begin to be his disciple, using his grace in you to help heal others who are blind as you used to be. Pray in gratitude for this tremendous gift.

Pray one Our Father, ten Hail Marys, one Glory Be.

The Fifth Decade

Then he sent him away to his home, saying, "Do not even go into the village." (Mark 8:26)

Meditation

Why would Jesus enjoin the man not to go back to the village? We know what it would have meant for Jesus at the time; over and over in these stories the Gospel writers portray Jesus as instructing the healed person not to talk about him, that he is not ready to be revealed as the Son of God. When we imagine how hard it is to keep ordinary good news to ourselves, we can imagine the torture it must have been for this man to keep his good news to himself. But what does it mean to us, who have the knowledge of the Resurrection and two thousand years of Christian history behind us?

If we see this healing as the proper restoration of our personal power and our ability to see ourselves in Christ, we also have to admit that many inner and outer temptations used to feed our blindness. Just as recovered addicts must take time away from their old haunts, we have to take time off from our old ways of "seeing" ourselves and from the habits that have taken root in our hearts and minds. We have to be braver in admitting how our illness and unease of mind sometimes served us when we did not have the strength or wisdom to face reality. We have to admit that often we relied on our blindness to make things easier. We need not completely uproot our old lives or reject our family and friends. We do, however, need to abandon our old interior habits of thinking, because we are, in fact, experiencing a conversion of sight and heart.

How do we do this? We first continue to put our trust in the fact that Jesus will continue to help us not be afraid to see what he wants us to see. We then begin to live "as if" this is already happening. As you begin this final decade—and each time you return to this prayer—imagine and remember: Imagine how the darkness was replaced by the light. Imagine that first glimpse of things in the world. Imagine the beautiful face of Jesus by your side. Remember what you have seen. Remember to rejoice in the graces of having come this far. Remember to tell Jesus again and again that he has healed you to see.

Pray one Our Father, ten Hail Marys, one Glory Be.

End the decade by praying the Hail, Holy Queen, or other prayer to the Blessed Virgin Mary.

End of the Second Healing Mystery

PART THREE

Jesus Raises Us
to New Life

The Raising of Jairus's Daughter.
(Mark 5:22–24; 35–43)

Opening Reflection

*T*his mystery has to do with wounds to our spirit and courage, and the actual fear we all have of what it will mean to end this life. It is a story told about a young girl who has "fallen asleep." We can see this as a metaphor for what happens to many of us in modern life. So many people in our society remain on the threshold of adulthood, standing in a place somewhere in the middle, not quite living their lives fully even as they pass through their middle years into old age. The process of growing up—and staying in our adult selves—seems to terrify us. Meeting the demands of adulthood—the demands of commitment, of commu-

nity, and of sexuality–are not givens for us in the twenty-first century.

In today's culture, sexuality in particular is not only identified with youth, it is also becoming increasingly marketed to children. The way sexuality is perceived, with the increasing sexualization of children, can cause adolescents and young adults to look for ways to avoid having to cross the threshold of adulthood and maturity. Young women, instead of looking forward to maturing into womanhood, try any means to forestall it; they see their mothers take drastic measures to reverse or erase the passage of time. Young men experiment with ever more violent and self-destructive behavior as a substitute for paths they cannot find or embrace that will lead them to true manhood. They arrive at middle age still needing to forestall the inevitable decline of life and reality of physical death.

Along the way, both men and women are tempted from all sides to try to "go back" to that time when they imagined there was a clarity about themselves and their place in the world, usually a time before they began to feel the pressure of a distorted sexuality or of the fear of the real burdens and responsibilities that maturation brings.

As we progress through adulthood, many of us begin a search for ways to "fall asleep" and stay there. Better to be asleep in life than to face the pain of death. Dissociated from this life in this way, we can hardly rejoice in the hope of the life that waits after this. We waste, we squander, and ultimately, when youth and energy are spent, we are left empty. Death appears as the enemy, and it seems sure that death will win. We may desire to end our life, and some people do. Those who don't may become stuck in a place "in between," a flat life of going through the motions or one bound in depression or anger. We tire out our loved ones or push them away. We develop sicknesses that don't heal. We turn away from God because he seems to have left us. This beautiful story from Mark reminds us of what can be had now and of what is to come.

It is striking that Jairus, one of the rulers of the synagogue, cannot help his own daughter. He cannot raise her to life, and she cannot hear his voice; whatever has happened has put her beyond her father's help. Jairus seeks out Jesus to raise her, and he is not disappointed. Jesus reassures him that she is not dead; she is only sleeping the sleep of one who cannot wake up by herself. Jesus comes to her, calls her daughter, tells her she can get up. She finds in his voice what she could not hear in any other. In him she finds her way back to life.

As you begin this mystery, imagine yourself lying in that bed; hearing as if from a long distance the noise of the crowd; breathing the thick, dusty air; and somewhere inside your sleep holding onto the hope that, even though you are alone, even though you are feeling death, life and its goodness are not over for you. Imagine what is to come; imagine the time when you will be free, free to truly awaken to a new life that will last forever.

The First Decade

Then one of the leaders of the synagogue named Jairus came and, when he saw him, fell at his feet, and begged him repeatedly, saying, "My little daughter is at the point of death. Come and lay your hands on her, so that she may be made well, and live." So he went with him. (Mark 5:22-24)

Meditation

Jairus speaks for the community in which he lives. He has power to direct people's lives, and the wisdom to lead people to God. We have the sense that he is a righteous man, a good man who loves his daughter, and we feel his anguish in his inability to reach her. As parents, we understand what it means to want to speak words that will end our children's struggles. As children, we understand what it means to want to hear those words. If our parents have ever betrayed us, we know how it feels to experience the things they say as potential betrayals. If we have been betrayed by our church, or if the words of our church leaders can't reach us, that despair can be equally great.

If we find solace in sleep—the sleep of illness, of quiet, or merely escape—sleep may seem to be the answer, and it may actually help for a time. As you begin to pray this decade, remember what led you to let go and fall asleep. But then imagine that you are beginning to turn away from sleep and toward life. Begin to hear, as if far in the distance, the sound of Jesus on his way to you, accompanied by those whom you love most. Imagine that soon he'll be with you, bringing the gift of a life worth living.

Pray one Our Father, ten Hail Marys, one Glory Be.

The Second Decade

> *While he was still speaking, some people came from the leader's house to say, "Your daughter is dead. Why trouble the teacher any further?" But overhearing what they said, Jesus said to the leader of the synagogue, "Do not fear, only believe." (Mark 5:35–36)*

Meditation

In our sleep it is hard and sometimes impossible to remember that there are others who love us and who are working and praying for us. Perhaps we may hear only voices like those from Jairus's house, voices that proclaim we are beyond help, already dead, not worth troubling God about. Perhaps we are asking the same question they are: "Why trouble Jesus any longer?" But Jesus is there, telling us firmly to turn away from this temptation.

Imagine that as you lie on the bier, you hear only the wailing and despair of those who mourn your death. You are afraid, you have no idea what will follow. Now imagine the din of this mourning begins to fade. Suddenly it is quiet. Next you find that you can hear Jesus in the distance, telling your loved ones, "Do not fear, only believe." Remember as you begin to pray this decade that you have advocates all

around you, even in the community of saints. They are praying for you to get up, even as you and others are tempted to
give in to your death. Remember and believe: You are not
already dead, you are still here. Jesus is near. Repeat as often
as you need, "Do not fear, only believe."

Pray one Our Father, ten Hail Marys, one Glory Be.

The Third Decade

*When they came to the house of the leader of
the synagogue, he saw a commotion, people
weeping and wailing loudly. When he had
entered, he said to them, "Why do make a
commotion and weep? The child is not dead
but sleeping." (Mark 5:38–39)*

Meditation

We have come to believe that we are alone, that
whoever sees us sees someone already gone. But Jesus tells
us the truth: we are only asleep! The ones who are weeping for us cannot see us correctly. Perhaps they are afraid
of losing us, or afraid of their own fears and needs, and of
what our illness reminds them. When they mirror a false
and painful image of ourselves to us, we may come to
believe in it in many ways, but still hope they are wrong.
Eventually we cannot bear the noise of their grief; we avoid
them and "go under" to a place where it seems we will be
safe. We must let Jesus come in now, before the sleepy
pleasure of not having to live takes us over.

Again imagine that now you can hear Jesus' voice

even more clearly than the din of those mourning around you. Ask what it is that you yourself are hiding from, what you would "make a commotion and weep" over if you were not asleep. Then imagine the indescribable relief you begin to feel, now that Jesus has entered your house. Imagine the kind of trembling of body that is the thrill of joy, and know that it is about to be yours, regardless of whatever else is happening to you. Tell yourself that you are alive. Imagine you are about to get up, Jesus at your side.

Pray one Our Father, ten Hail Marys, one Glory Be.

The Fourth Decade

And they laughed at him. Then he put them all outside, and took the child's father and mother and those who were with him, and went in where the child was. He took her by the hand and said to her, "Talitha cum," which means, "Little girl, get up!" (Mark 5:40–41)

Meditation

Of all the moments of healing in the Gospel, this is among the most beautiful and wonderful. Even though we are now adults, such a big part of us feels like that little girl still on the threshold of adulthood! We still need a protector. We need to hear someone call to us, someone who understands that inside we are indeed vulnerable and afraid. We need our protector's loving arm around us. We need our friend to help us get to the next place, unalone, unafraid.

Imagine how you can hear the people laugh in derision at Jesus' faith in your life. Let this firm your resolve not to rejoin them. But then sense how Jesus takes over their hearts. Suddenly, it is not only Jesus, but everyone you love or have ever loved who comes for you. Jesus knows you can still get up, he calls you by name, and he shows your loved ones how to help you and be with you. He tells them: Be gentle with her, believe in her, and she will get up. Your heart fills with indescribable happiness; your grief and fear leave you; you are with your friends.

Now imagine how near Jesus is to you at this very moment. Feel the excitement in taking his hand, anticipate rising from that bed of illusion. Imagine the joy of your loved ones when they are reunited with you! Above all, imagine how Jesus will continue to care for that frightened part of yourself and to gently reassure you when life feels too difficult to face.

Pray one Our Father, ten Hail Marys, one Glory Be.

The Fifth Decade

And immediately the girl got up and began to walk about (she was twelve years of age). At this they were overcome with amazement. He strictly ordered that no one should know this, and told them to give her something to eat. (Mark 5:42–43)

Meditation

Imagine now what it would be like to be able to claim your true self in the fullness of your life, and that when you get up, you will receive the nourishment you need, the encouragement to go forward, and the knowledge of why you are alive in the world. Compared to how you felt before, how amazed you will be! How differently you will look at your life now and the life that is still to come.

Now see and feel: The cloth over your head is being lifted; the warm air of the dusty room has become a comfort instead of a distress. You get up—you do the thing you thought you could not do—and you are not afraid. Your loved ones are silent for a moment, then the room fills with noise, but this time with the excitement of a birthday or coming-of-age party. Imagine the joy at seeing Jesus there beside you. Imagine the faces of your loved ones as they welcome you back from your sleep. Imagine someone handing you a plate of delicious food, and hovering over you as you take in good nourishment, little by little.

Then think of the very next thing that you will do, and the next, and the next after that. Feel ease in your limbs and courage in your heart. Imagine the joy of Jesus as he sees you get up, knowing that he wants nothing from you but your happiness. Finally, begin to feel a readiness to move on in the world, Jesus and those you love by your side. Know that you are not now, and will never be, alone. Trust completely how much you are connected to all of creation, how completely you are loved, safe, and healed.

Believe in this foretaste of the promise of eternal life. Move on to love as you truly have been loved.

Pray one Our Father, ten Hail Marys, one Glory Be.

End the decade by praying the Hail, Holy Queen, or other prayer to the Blessed Virgin.

End of the Third Healing Mystery

APPENDIX:
The Order of the Rosary

Make the Sign of the Cross:

    In the name of the Father, and of the Son, and of the Holy Spirit. Amen

Holding the crucifix, say the **Apostles' Creed:**

    I believe in God, the Father almighty, creator of heaven and earth. I believe in Jesus Christ, his only Son, our Lord. He was conceived by the power of the Holy Spirit and born of the Virgin Mary. He suffered under Pontius Pilate, was crucified, died, and was buried. He descended into hell. On the third day he rose again. He ascended into heaven and is seated at the right hand of the Father. He will come again to judge the living and the dead. I believe in the Holy Spirit, the holy catholic Church, the communion of saints, the forgiveness of sins, the resurrection of the body, and the life everlasting. Amen.

On the first bead, say the **Our Father:**

Our Father who art in heaven, hallowed be thy name. Thy kingdom come. Thy will be done on earth, as it is in heaven. Give us this day our daily bread, and forgive us our trespasses, as we forgive those who trespass against us, and lead us not into temptation, but deliver us from evil. Amen.

On each of the next three beads, say the **Hail Mary:**

Hail Mary, full of grace, the Lord is with thee; blessed art thou among women, and blessed is the fruit of thy womb, Jesus. Holy Mary, Mother of God, pray for us sinners, now and at the hour of our death. Amen.

On the last bead of those following the crucifix, say the **Doxology (Glory Be):**

Glory be to the Father, and to the Son, and to the Holy Spirit. As it was in the beginning, is now, and ever shall be, world without end. Amen.

Next, read the opening reflection of the healing mystery you are praying. Follow this reflection by reading the scripture passage and meditation for the first decade that follows it. Pray the Our Father, followed by ten Hail Marys (on the ten beads of the first decade). On the single bead that separates the first decade from the second, pray the Glory Be.

If you continue on, repeat this sequence: read the scripture passage and meditation for the second decade, then pray the Our Father on the same separating bead that you prayed the ending Glory Be of the decade before. Pray the Hail Mary on each of the next ten beads, and conclude with the Glory Be on the next separating bead.

Repeat this sequence until you have completed the fifth decade.

End the healing mystery by praying the **Salve Regina (Hail Holy Queen):**

Hail, Holy Queen, Mother of Mercy, our life, our sweetness, and our hope! To thee we cry, poor banished children of Eve; to thee do we send up our sighs, mourning, and weeping in this valley of tears. Turn then, most gracious advocate, thine eyes of mercy toward us, and after this our exile, show us the blessed fruit of thy womb, Jesus. O clement, O loving, O sweet virgin Mary! Pray for us, O Holy Mother of God, that we may be made worthy of the promises of Christ. Amen.

Other prayers to the Blessed Virgin include:

Loving mother of the redeemer, Gate of Heaven, Star of the Sea, assist your people who have fallen yet strive to rise again. To the wonderment of nature you bore your Creator, yet remained a virgin after as before. You, who received Gabriel's joyful greeting, have mercy on us.

The Memorare of Saint Bernard

Remember, O most gracious Virgin Mary, that never was it known that anyone who fled to thy protection, implored thy help, or sought thy intercession was left unaided. Inspired with this confidence, I fly unto thee, O Virgin of virgins, my mother: to thee do I come, before thee I stand, sinful and sorrowful. O Mother of the Word Incarnate, despise not my petitions, but in thy mercy hear and answer me. Amen.

In your loving care we take refuge, O holy Mother of God. Do not disregard our prayers in the time of our need, but set us free from every danger, O glorious and blessed Virgin.

Notes

1. In terms of the traditional form and prayers of the Rosary, I was helped by several of the many excellent resources that can be found in any religious bookstore. If you also need a refresher on how to pray the traditional Rosary, or if praying with a Rosary is altogether new to you, the proper order and text of each prayer is listed for convenience at the end of the book. In the section "Recommended Readings," Caryll Houselander's *The Essential Rosary* is also an excellent and beautiful resource.

2. *Of utmost importance:* This is not a book on spiritual direction nor is it intended in any way to take the place of professional guidance. If you are new to prayer and have any anxiety or discomfort in the course of your prayer (whether this or any other), don't go it alone! Find a reliable companion as you begin: a trusted pastor, spiritual director, or knowledgeable friend with whom you can talk as the need arises.

Further, if you are the victim of sexual or other abuse (especially if you have not begun or are in the early stages of recovery), please consider getting professional help with someone skilled in the treatment of this kind of trauma. Parents United has many chapters across the country that can provide resources of support to adult survivors of sexual abuse. The Sidran Institute, located on the web at www.sidran.org, also has many resources available for people who have suffered a wide variety of traumatic experiences, including those associated with domestic violence.

3. An outstanding reference for this concept can be found in Judith L. Hermann, *Trauma and Recovery*, rev. ed. (New York: Basic Books, 1997). Although somewhat technical, the book addresses the problems of trauma from many perspectives, including domestic abuse, combat trauma, and forced confinement and/or torture (chronic painful illness can also result in many of the same effects as other traumas). Hermann's thesis is that there are three components essential to recovery: recovery of safety, revisiting and grieving the trauma, and reconnecting with the greater community (reestablishing one's relationship with God and one's faith community would be included here). The method of prayer in Healing Mysteries is largely concerned with reconnecting, the third phase of recovery, but certainly can be used at any point.

4. This feeling of existential emptiness is very difficult to address because it takes place in a culture which exploits and encourages that feeling to the point of identifying it with reality. See Ronald Rolheiser, *The Shattered Lantern: Rediscovering a Felt Presence of God*, rev. ed. (New York: Crossroad, 2001) for a response to this cultural attitude; especially Part 1, on the widespread phenomenon of "unbelief among believers."

5. For this insight into how God is present in our lives, I am especially indebted to Fr. Richard Hauser, SJ, director of the

Creighton University Christian Spirituality Program, and Sr. Marie Louise Flick, RSCJ, instructor in the program and spiritual director at the Spiritual Ministry Center in San Diego, California.

6. An excellent treatment of this cultural perspective is found in Richard Hauser, SJ, *In His Spirit: A Guide to Today's Spirituality* (Mahwah, NJ: Paulist Press, 1986).

7. Richard O'Connor, *Undoing Depression: What Therapy Doesn't Teach You and Medication Can't Give You,* rev. ed. (Berkeley, CA: Berkeley Publishing Group, 1999), pp. 29–33.

8. Periods of "consolation" followed by ones of "desolation" are understood by spiritual directors as graces from God and are considered normal fluctuations within the course of a maturing spiritual and prayer life. A sound discussion of this dynamic (although the authors do not use the same vocabulary) can be found in The Monks of New Skete, *In the Spirit of Happiness: Wisdom for Living* (London: Rider, 2000). However, in cases of traumatic injury or illness, I would argue with Carl Jung that a spiritual malaise sets in, one that becomes quite different from the natural changes in experience of God. To *never* feel God's presence or love in one's life is a very difficult problem, not a normal course of events for the believer, and requires companionship and guidance to heal.

9. Again, many thanks to Sr. Marie Louise Flick for several of these suggestions.

Suggested Reading

Brock, Rita Nakashima, and Rebecca Ann Parker. *Proverbs of Ashes: Violence, Redemptive Suffering and the Search for What Saves Us.* Boston: Beacon Press, 2001.

Callahan, Rachel, and Rea McDonnell. *God Is Close to the Brokenhearted: Good News for Those Who Are Depressed.* Cincinnati: St. Anthony Messenger Press, 1996.

Fiand, Barbara. *Prayer and the Quest for Healing.* New York: Crossroad Publishing Company, 1999.

Flanigan, Beverly. *Forgiving the Unforgivable: Overcoming the Bitter Legacy of Intimate Wounds.* New York: Macmillan, 1992.

Frankl, Viktor E. *Man's Search for Meaning: An Introduction to Logotherapy.* 3rd ed. New York: Simon and Schuster, 1984.

Hauser, Richard J. *Finding God in Troubled Times: The Holy Spirit and Suffering.* New York/Mahwah, NJ: Paulist Press, 1995.

Houselander, Caryll. *The Essential Rosary*. Manchester, NH: The Sophia Institute Press, 1996.

Leech, Kenneth. *True Prayer: An Invitation to Christian Spirituality*. Harrisburg, PA: Morehouse Publishing, 1986.

Malina, Bruce J. and Richard L. Rohrbaugh. *Social Science Commentary on the Synoptic Gospels*. 2nd ed. Minneapolis: Fortress Press, 2003.

Monks of Glenstal Abbey. *The Glenstal Book of Prayer: A Benedictine Prayer Book*. Collegeville, MN: The Liturgical Press, 2001.

Rohlheiser, Ronald. *The Holy Longing: The Search for a Christian Spirituality*. New York: Doubleday, 1999.

Watkins, James D., comp. *Manual of Prayers*. 3rd ed. Chicago: Midwest Theological Forum, 1998.

ILLUMINATIONBOOKS

Other Books in the Series

Little Pieces of Light...Darkness and Personal Growth
  by Joyce Rupp

Joy, The Dancing Spirit of Love Surrounding You
  by Beverly Elaine Eanes

Why Are You Worrying?
  by Joseph W. Ciarrocchi

Appreciating God's Creation Through Scripture
  by Alice L. Laffey

Let Yourself Be Loved
  by Phillip Bennett

Living Simply in an Anxious World
  by Robert J. Wicks

A Rainy Afternoon with God
  by Catherine B. Cawley

Time, A Collection of Fragile Moments
  by Joan Monahan

15 Ways to Nourish Your Faith
  by Susan Shannon Davies

God Lives Next Door
  by Lyle K. Weiss

Hear the Just Word & Live It
　　　by Walter J. Burghardt, S.J.

The Love That Keeps Us Sane
　　　by Marc Foley, O.C.D.

The Threefold Way of Saint Francis
　　　by Murray Bodo, O.F.M.

Everyday Virtues
　　　by John W. Crossin, O.S.F.S.

The Mysteries of Light
　　　by Roland J. Faley

Carrying the Cross with Christ
　　　by Joseph T. Sullivan